AROUND
WILTON
IN OLD PHOTOGRAPHS

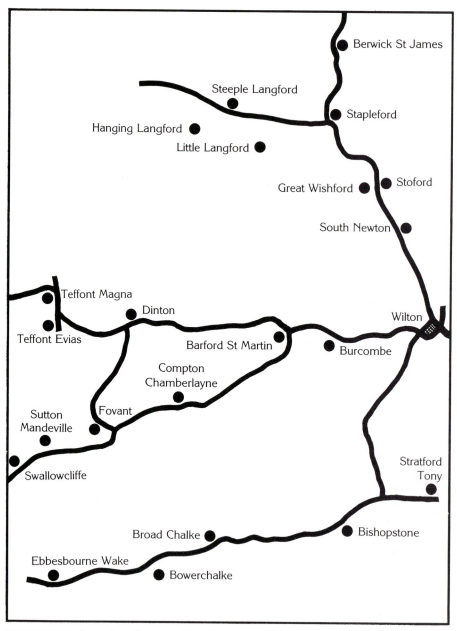

Berwick St James

Steeple Langford

Stapleford

Hanging Langford

Little Langford

Great Wishford   Stoford

South Newton

Teffont Magna

Dinton   Wilton

Teffont Evias

Barford St Martin   Burcombe

Compton
Chamberlayne

Fovant

Sutton
Mandeville

Stratford
Tony

Swallowcliffe

Broad Chalke   Bishopstone

Ebbesbourne Wake

Bowerchalke

THE MAP ABOVE shows the villages and hamlets around Wilton which are included in this, the latest album of old photographs to have been compiled by Peter Daniels. The areas to the north and east of Wilton are covered in three companion volumes, all by the same author: *Salisbury, Around Salisbury* and *Around Amesbury*. (The map is not to scale.)

AROUND
WILTON
IN OLD PHOTOGRAPHS

COLLECTED BY
PETER DANIELS

ALAN SUTTON

Alan Sutton Publishing Limited
Phoenix Mill · Far Thrupp · Stroud · Gloucestershire

First published 1991

British Library Cataloguing in Publication Data

Around Wilton in old photographs.
I. Daniels, Peter, *1948–*
942.319

ISBN 0-86299-931-6

Typeset in 9/10 Korinna.
Typesetting and origination by
Alan Sutton Publishing Limited.
Printed in Great Britain by
The Bath Press, Avon.

CONTENTS

PETER DANIELS, 'THE OLD PICTURE DETECTIVE', seen here with a 1948 Field Marshall Contractor from the Christopher Lodge Collection. The picture was taken at Samways Farm, Alvediston in July 1991. (Photograph courtesy of Russell Emm)

INTRODUCTION

Around Wilton in Old Photographs is the fourth book in the series to feature the south-east corner of Wiltshire. Compiled by Peter Daniels, all are illustrated with pictures taken from the earliest days of photography to within thirty years of the present day. Nothing brings about more change than time itself so it is inevitable that many changes have taken place around the towns and villages since the Victorian era. This evocative collection of old photographs records what has been and gone, as well as what remains, albeit in an altered form. The pictures will provoke memories for many and be a source of enlightenment to others.

The photographers of yesteryear, both amateur and professional, captured the various aspects of life through their camera lenses without realizing that in years to come their prints would be the only visual record of a particular person, place or event. These are real moments, frozen in time. Their task was not an easy one, and we can only imagine now what it was like to cycle many miles around the countryside with boxes of heavy glass plate negatives, a tripod and a large mahogany camera. Our vision of these characters is greatly enhanced by the pictures of Charlie May and Albert Marett which appear on p. 19. One cannot help but wonder how many of today's scenes would be recognized by those early photographers if it were possible for them to make a return visit. Probably no more than a few. Many old buildings have been pulled down and modern structures put in their place. Roads and bridges have been widened and new highways constructed. Similarly, they would never have seen before the host of features which we all take for granted these days, such as telephone cables, television aerials and electricity pylons.

The photographs in section four give us an insight into the days before the telephone, when all messages were passed by the village carrier or postman. The golden era of the picture postcard was between 1903 and the First World War, the peak years being around 1906–7, when a daily average of more than ten thousand cards was posted, Sundays included, and unlike today even the smallest community had its own post office. Some were quite impressive affairs, incorporated with the village general store. An equal number, however, were more humble concerns, and possibly just a single room in what was, in all outward appearances, a private cottage. Both extremes can be seen in the section starting on p. 53.

The commercial aspects of life are depicted in the sections devoted to work and transport, where a wide selection of road vehicles are shown. In the distant days of the last century man's best friend and servant was the horse, the motive power for a copious collection of conveyances including charabancs, traps, and goods and agricultural vehicles. A few pioneering examples of transport from a new era, the age of the motor car, are represented. Few of the roads on which they travelled were metalled and many were nothing more than dirt tracks, dusty in the summer and muddy in the winter. Maintenance was just as important then as it is now, however, and within the pages of this book one can see the road gangs of Fovant and Wilton who worked so hard to keep the surfaces of our highways in a good state of repair. Another significant change to our transportation habits was brought about by the completion of the railway networks during the second half of the last century. In addition to the two railway stations at Wilton, there were smaller stations at Dinton and Wishford. Sadly, these have been closed down, and in some cases the only evidence that they ever existed are a few grass-covered platforms. Industry is represented by the Dinton brick works, the Wilton carpet factory and the Wilton felt mill, where several different stages of production are shown. These factories and the Wilton sheep fairs are all reminders of a long association with the wool trade, but probably never again will we be able to see flocks of sheep being driven through the streets. Nowadays the sheep arrive at Wilton Fair Field in motor lorries instead of being transported by train. The principal employment in the area was agriculture and many delightful scenes of farming life are included in the section headed 'All in a Day's Work'.

It did not make a great deal of difference whether an individual worked in the factory or the field; he or she was expected to work long and hard, and the majority did. They certainly deserved their leisure time, which was used to the full, as recorded in section eight, 'Memorable Events'. Life has its sad moments too and pictures of floods and funerals are included.

The changing face of fashion can be followed: Edwardian ladies are pictured in their full-length skirts, puffed-sleeve blouses and flower bedecked hats. Their menfolk, not quite so concerned about their general appearance, wore a hat or cap appropriate to the season and time of day.

Peter Daniels is to be commended for putting together this wonderful selection of old photographs. Even after a brief glimpse one can clearly see why he is known as the 'Old Picture Detective'. Let us all hope that there will be people like him in the future who will collect and research images of the latter years of the twentieth century. It would be nice for our children's children to be taken back to the days of their grandparents in the way that we are in the pages of this delightful book.

Pat Brown
August 1991

SECTION ONE

Village Folk

THE ASHFORD FAMILY at Little Bathampton Farm in 1904. Sis, Dolly, Madge and Challis can be seen in the back row with their father Edward James Ashford. Bess, Ann Challis (Edward's wife) and Jim are sitting in the middle row, and Clara, Pidgeon and Tallie are on the rug. Edward is pictured with his very rare Chase motorcycle, AM 407. Only a relatively small number of these were made by Chase Brothers of London between 1904 and 1906.

THE BURT AND HOSKINS FAMILIES at Swallowcliffe in 1914. Polly and John Burt are at the back of the group, surrounded by their children. Harold, Stan and Dorothy are to the left and Daisy is in front, next to her husband, George Hoskins. Harold is sitting on his mother's lap.

PRIVATE EDWARD SIMPER OF FOVANT. During the First World War 'Ted' served with 1st Platoon, A-Company, 7th Battalion, Wiltshire Regiment (service number 12240). He and Tommy Riggs were the first of Fovant's boys who left home to join Kitchener's army. A woodman for the Earl of Pembroke, he lived at Ivy Cottage. Ted was one of the lucky ones, for he returned home, and in 1921 married Lucy Raymond of Sutton Mandeville.

ONE BIG HAPPY FAMILY at Farm Orchard, Sutton Mandeville, in around 1905. Frank and Margaret Mullins can be seen here with their daughter Dorothy, ten of their eleven sons, four daughters-in-law and two grandchildren. Which son is missing, Alfred, Edward, Frank Junior, Fred, Gilbert, Harry, James, Sidney, Thomas, Walter or William?

THE WYATT FAMILY of Compton Chamberlayne, pictured here in the orchard behind their cottage. The three children at the back are Elsie, Dora and 'Jim'. Left to right in the front row is Frances, William, William Junior, Frances (née Pringle), John and Florence. Some years ago this photograph brightened up a wall in Dinton post office.

THE HABGOOD FAMILY at Bowerchalke post office in 1911. Kathleen stands to the left beside her mother Sara, William is at the back behind Elsie, and Isaac and Victoria are to the right. Isaac was a sub-postmaster and postman for more than sixty years and in 1954 he was the oldest postman in England. He died in 1956 at the age of eighty-eight.

THE CHALKE FAMILY of South Newton. Pictured from the left: Frederick (George); Herbert Cyril (Dick); Ciss; William Ewart (Joe); Ann (née Shergold); Freda; Walter Mark Chalke; and Leslie. The photograph was taken at around the time of the First World War.

THE KENT FAMILY at Croucheston Mill House. The photograph was taken in 1919 to mark the return of the boys from the Great War. William, Alan, Roy, Ernest, Maurice and Leonard are at the back. Winifred, Florence, Maud, Sidney, Eliza, Jessie and Doris are seated, and Sylvia and Rozalie are on the sheepskin rug.

BY THE BLOSSOMS at Broad Chalke. Pictured here in 1934 on the lawn at Reddish House is gardener Charles Penny, his wife Florence, their son Reginald and an unidentified toddler. Robert Wood lived here at this time, but by 1950 it was the residence of distinguished photographer Cecil Beaton.

BROAD CHALKE CHILDREN. Brothers Morgan and Reginald Emm (aged six and eight respectively) are pictured here with ten-year-old Timna Beatrice Emm and her little sister Irene. The photograph was taken at the Plough, Mount Sorrell, in 1905. We cannot name the seven-year-old girl to the left, do you recognize her?

COLONEL CHARLES S. COLLISON DSO, 1871–1935. Before taking up residence at the newly restored Rectory House at Stratford Tony in 1926, Colonel Collison was living with his wife Geraldine in Ireland. During his years in Wiltshire, Charles spent many enjoyable hours producing sketches of his neighbourhood, nineteen of which were later reproduced in a book. If you are lucky, and carry out a thorough search of the shelves of an antiquarian bookshop, you may just find a copy of *Sketches Near Salisbury*.

THE MISSES SIDFORD at Knighton in 1897. Nell and Vi can be seen here with a donkey at Knighton Manor Farm. Their father George Sidford was a tenant farmer for many years.

JOSEPH AND EMME on their wedding day. Soon after he married Emme Davis in 1904, Joseph Jesse Gurd took over the licence of the Railway Tavern at Hanging Langford. Some eight years later, however, they had moved to the Bell Inn at Steeple Langford and by 1920 they were managing the Royal Oak at Great Wishford.

THE BLAKE FAMILY of Barford St Martin in around 1900. Arthur H. Blake (village carrier) and Emily are pictured here with their seven children. Edwin is at the back to the left, Harry is next, then Elsie, Reginald and his wife Jean. Christine and Archibald are sitting at the front. The picture was probably taken at Greystones Cottage.

ARTHUR 'A.G.' STREET, 1892–1966. An accomplished gentleman, farmer, writer, broadcaster and lecturer. During the First World War A.G. took over the tenancy of Ditchampton Farm, which he kept until 1951. The first of his thirty-five books, *Farmer's Glory*, was published in 1932, and for many years he was a popular panel member on the long-running radio series, *Any Questions?*

THE REVEREND EDWARD COLLETT, 1847–1924, vicar of Bowerchalke for forty-six years, from 1878 until his death. He was a practised photographer, and for over forty years was publisher of the village news sheet. His series had reached 1,703 editions when production ceased in April 1922. If you would like to learn more about this remarkable man then we suggest that you read Rex Sawyer's delightful book, *The Bowerchalke Parish Papers* (Alan Sutton, 1989).

HENRY ANDREWS, 1836–1929. Born at Upton Lovell in Dorset, Mr Andrews moved to Standlynch, Wiltshire in 1855, where he remained for five years. He then farmed at Wishford and Wylye before moving to Little Langford Farm in 1874. Simultaneously, between 1882 and 1900, he managed Homanton Farm, Maddington (1882–95) and Eastcliffe Farm, Steeple Langford (1894–1900). He retired in 1920 and returned to Upton Lovell with his wife Mary Emma (née Flower). His sons took on two of the farms: Edgar was at Steeple Langford from around 1900; and Fred was at Little Langford from 1906. Later on Edgar's son, Donald, took on Eastcliffe Farm.

THE PEOPLE OF ANSTY AND SWALLOWCLIFFE on an outing to Brook, Hampshire, in 1923. The revellers are pictured here in The Canal, Salisbury where they stopped for a short break on the outward journey. George, Harold, Roy and Tom Hoskins can be seen in the group, also Polly Burt, Walter Coombes, Ern Oborne and George Viney. Can you find them?

CHARLES HENRY MAY, photographer, 1907. During the very early years of this century 'Charlie' lived at William Selway's dairy farm at Gomeldon Hill, Porton, although by 1910 he had moved to Swanwick, Hampshire. For many years he travelled around Wiltshire, Hampshire and Dorset, recording images of life in the towns and the villages. A few of his photographs appear in this book.

ALBERT FELTHAM MARETT, photographer, 1909. Born at Shrewton in November 1880, Albert produced thousands of Wiltshire photographs between 1909 and 1916. We are delighted that many of his prints have survived, including views of Berwick St James, the Langfords, Shrewton, Stapleford, Tilshead and the Salisbury Plain military camps.

A COMFORTABLE HOME at Grovely Wood. Jesse Gurd (1867–1945) is pictured here with his mother-in-law Sarah Davis and daughter Marjorie (later Mrs Head). During the early 1920s Jesse was the landlord of the Royal Oak Inn at Great Wishford, which can be seen on p. 72, and on p. 16 you will find a picture of him on the day he married Emme Davis. The photograph above was reproduced from two faded snapshots that had been cleverly spliced together. You can see the join.

People of the Town

THE COUNTESS OF PEMBROKE and friends. On 15 April 1925 a bazaar was held in the grounds of Bulbridge House to raise money for parochial church funds. It does appear, however, that the event was poorly attended and the profits amounted to just a few shillings. The Countess can be seen here giving her opening speech and Revd Guy Campbell, pictured third from the right, looks exceedingly bored with the proceedings, as his arms are folded and his head is drooping almost as if he was asleep.

ALICE FOYLE with seven children. Francis can be seen at the back between Cecily and Lilian (right). Gertrude is on the extreme left next to Edith, and Sidney is to the right. The youngest child is Vera (later Mrs A.G. Street). The head of the family was Francis Henry Foyle, who was a foreman at Wilton Felt Mill until the time of his death in 1918.

WILLIAM JUKES, photographer, printer and postcard publisher. A native of Gillingham, he came to Wilton in around 1896 to set up a new business at 91 North Street. For some time he was honorary overseer of the poor for the Wilton Union. His only hobby was bowls, being a founder member of Wilton Bowling Club. He married Edith Stone, who was also a native of Gillingham. He died on 14 January 1946 when in his seventy-fourth year. He left six children and nine grandchildren.

THE CHILDREN OF WILLIAM AND EDITH JUKES. In descending order, the picture above shows Cyril, Len, Stella, Ivy, Lily (later Mrs Foster) and Regy, who can be seen in the perambulator. We believe that the children were photographed by their father at the back of the family home and printing works at 91 North Street (the street numbering system had changed by 1955 and the house became number 2 North Street and the workshop, number 4). It was Len who took over the family business after the death of his father. The ornate baby carriage, incidentally, was often used as a prop when William was taking portrait photographs. A delightful picture of Edith has been reproduced on p. 119.

MEMBERS OF WILTON BOWLING CLUB in the 1930s. Left to right, in the back row: Messrs Farewell; Jukes; Dodge; Davis; Cross; Sinca; Houldridge; Mitchell; Robinson; and Storey. Next row: Harvey; Laidlaw; Elliott; E. Musselwhite; Burroughs; Kent(?) and F. Musselwhite. Everall and Love are in front.

THE PRIDE OF MR KENDLE. In June 1909 George Robert Kendle was presented with an award for growing this colossal cucumber. It was 47 inches in length, had a circumference of almost 12 inches, and it weighed 9 pounds. Mr Kendle was a land agent to the Earl of Pembroke, and his office was in South Street.

BILL STROUD, Wilton's youngest hero. On Saturday 9 May 1908 William Thomas Stroud rescued his friend Reginald Payne who had slipped and fallen into the River Nadder at Ugford. The unfortunate lad could not swim and would certainly have drowned. It took Bill nearly an hour to revive his playmate who was unconscious after being under water for several minutes. Bill is pictured here with the award that was presented to him by the Royal Humane Society.

THE WILTON SUNDAY SCHOOL SUMMER TREAT, 1908. Held at Street's Park, at the lower end of the Grovely Road. Every banner displayed here has a different message. 'Come unto Jesus' and 'God is Light' are two examples.

ISAAC MOORE, great-great-grandfather of Mrs Nancy Morland, who was Mayor of Wilton 1990/1. Born at Wilton in 1792, he was baptized at the Crow Lane chapel. He was a cloth weaver by trade and a local Wesleyan Methodist preacher. He died of a chill soon after getting caught out in a blizzard at South Newton in 1885.

OFFICERS OF WILTON BOROUGH COUNCIL, 1899. Left to right, in the front row: William Vincent Moore Jnr; -?-; William Vincent Moore Senior; Joseph W. Ward (mayor); John White; Edward Slow and John Moore. Henry Street (baker, grocer and farmer) is at the back of the group with Henry John King, who was town clerk.

CHARLES BUNDY AND FLORENCE MUNDY, who were married at St Paul's church, Salisbury, on 19 September 1923. Charles was born in Fancy Row, Wilton (the present site of Churchill Court) on 23 November 1898 to Thomas (a bricklayer) and Rose (née George) Bundy. For many years he was a policeman at Bulford.

FREDERICK THOMAS BLAKE in 1914. Christened with the first names of his father and grandfather, Frederick was born at Fancy Row, Wilton, on 25 March 1912, to Frederick Charles Blake and Emily Maud (née Bundy), Charles Bundy's sister. His first job was at the Wilton felt mills, but in later life he was a civil servant. Frederick's daughter, now Mrs Pat Brown, is very interested in Wilton history and several of the pictures in this book are from her collection.

CHARLES MITCHELL and family. Born in 1845, Charles was house steward to the 13th Earl of Pembroke and Montgomery from 1871 to 1895. He is pictured with his wife Ellen and daughters Elizabeth and Beatrice. He passed away in 1913.

'BUTTERCUP JOE' HORNE. We believe that this is the man who inspired A.G. Street's character Buttercup Joe, who appeared in his first book, *Farmer's Glory*, which was published in 1932. We are not too sure about Mr Horne's first name. Was it George or Thomas?

THE FIRST WILTON SCOUT TROOP, which reported to the District Association on 23 November 1911. The group was registered soon afterwards and a warrant was granted to Leonard Hinton, who was the master of Wilton national school. Do you recognize Capt. A.C. Randall (4th Wiltshire Regiment) or Ken Uphill?

CLARA JANE ELKINS AND CHARLES PALK LORAINE PRICE in 1880. It was love at first sight when Clara Jane called to have a portrait photograph taken by Charles at his studio in Hythe, Kent. They married soon afterwards and moved to Sherborne, Dorset, and eventually to The Poplars at Quidhampton. It was at this time that Charles opened a photographic studio in North Street, Wilton. Coincidentally, on the day that this caption was written, 2 August 1991, Clara's daughter 'Clarrie' was celebrating her 101st birthday.

A PORTRAIT OF MISS PIKE, 1906. Bessie Pike, later Mrs Harry Blake, came to Wilton in 1899 with her parents, Frank and Emma, who took over the Six Bells public house in North Street. Some time later, after her father had passed away, she took her mother to live in a neighbouring property known as Albany Cottage. In 1913 a shop opposite became available and Emma and Bessie took it on and started their own business. When Emma died in 1945, Bessie became the sole proprietor. For more details of the Pike family see pp. 121 and 125.

ONE FOR THE MEN ONLY. There were certainly a few females working at the Wilton felt mills in the 1920s and yet there is not one to be seen here. Equality for women was something for the future. The works foreman here for many years was Tip Turner, who died in 1955, aged seventy-five.

WAITING FOR THE KING, 27 June 1908. From their allocated place here in Minster Street the children of Wilton National School were able to get an unobstructed view of the King and Queen as they passed by *en route* to Wilton House.

THE ROYAL HOUSE PARTY. Standing, left to right: Marquis of Salisbury; Lord Revelstoke; Lord Herbert; Hon. Charlotte Knollys; Earl de Grey; Capt. Fortescue; Earl of Rosebery; Earl of Pembroke; HM The Queen; Countess of Pembroke; Earl of Durham; Capt. Wilkinson; Hon. George Herbert; Lady Muriel Herbert. Seated: Lady Herbert; Marchioness of Salisbury; Countess de Grey; HM The King; Marchioness of Lansdowne; Lady Beatrix Wilkinson; Marquis of Lansdowne.

SECTION THREE

All in a Day's Work

THE FELT MILL FIRE BRIGADE at Wilton during the late 1950s. Pictured here at the factory fire station, with appliances old and new, are Ronald Blake, Jim Goddard, Archie West and Bill Paddock. The ancient machine was entirely dependent on man, whereas the new Dennis trailer-pump had its own petrol-engined power source, which could quickly be towed to the fire ground by a motor tender.

E.V. NAISH'S FELT MILL, Wilton, in around 1900. The boys pictured here in the sheet carding machine shop all appear to be very young, indeed one or two of them look to be only about ten years of age. The firm was founded during the first decade of the last century and is still an important industry in the town. In 1859 the firm was included in a local trade directory: 'William Naish, Worsted Cord Manufacturer, Penny's Lane, Wilton'.

Right: ON TENTERHOOKS. The tentering machine pictured here was manufactured by Sellers of Huddersfield in 1953 and installed at the Crow Lane works some time later. After being stretched across hooks the felt was automatically drawn through this contrivance of steam-heated pipes where it was dried. Dick Best and Stan Penny were operating the machine when this picture was taken.

WARMTH, DAMPNESS AND MOVEMENT, the ideal environment in which to process felt. Taken in the early 1900s, this is a view of the hand felting shop where men worked in pairs to produce piano hammer felt. A large reliable steam engine was installed to keep the machines turning, including the drive-shaft, wheels and belts that can be seen in this picture.

THE FIRST CARPET MANUFACTORY in England was at Wilton, where many of the world's largest carpets were made. Ask any outlander what Wilton is most noted for and he or she will probably reply, 'its carpets'. Our picture of the factory, taken in around 1907, shows one of the power looms in the Wilton and Brussels section. At certain times during the 1800s nearly five hundred men and women were working here, and even in this new age there are around three hundred employees.

Right: A POWER LOOM at work in 1946. Over the last two hundred years there have been many names associated with the Wilton carpet factory: William Buller (late 1700s); Buller and Swatton (early 1800s); Blackmore Brothers (1820s); Lapworth Brothers (1860s); Blackmore and Lapworth (1870s) and Yates and Company (1880/90s). In 1905 a set of carpets was especially woven for King Edward VII, who then granted a royal warrant to the firm. Soon afterwards the company name was changed to Wilton Royal Carpet Factory Company Ltd.

HEAVY HORSES at Compton Chamberlayne. Taken during the First World War at Manor Farm, the photograph above shows six of William Langdon's powerful horses. The man pictured to the right is Joseph Langdon, who puts in a second appearance on p. 151.

A HORSE-DRAWN RING ROLLER at Henry Street's farm in 1913. The photograph shows Harry Matthews working on the land at Red Buildings, Ugford. Shortly after this picture was taken Harry moved to Upper Woodford to take on the job of head carter to The Hon. Louis Greville.

AT KNIGHTON, a job well done! In around 1890 this modest shooting party had been working at Knighton Manor Farm, Broad Chalke. Pictured here with their double-barrelled shotguns are George Sidford (left), Master Gulliver, his father George Gulliver, Harry Hitchings and Charlie Haimes.

GENTLE GIANTS at Barford St Martin in around 1918. Oddly enough we can name the carters but we do not know where the picture was taken. Fred Miles and Fred Penny are to the left and Frank Daniels is to the right. The third man is not the writer's late father; he just shared the same name.

A BUSY SCENE at Little Langford Farm before 1914. Albert Foot is the young lad pictured here turning the handle of a new sack hoist that was designed by Henry Andrews of Little Langford Farm, who can be seen on p. 18. The manufacturers of this labour-saving device were, among others, Brewer & Co. of Wilton and Armitage of Salisbury. Our picture shows that even a nine-year-old boy could load a wagon with 2 cwt sacks of grain when using Andrews' Patent Sack Elevator. The cost was just £6 5s.

TROOPER AND FRIENDS at Chilhampton Farm. Only six of William Hunt's ten heavy horses can be seen here. Warwick is to the left, then Trooper and head carter Albert Edward Brice, Ted Compton is in the centre and Herbie Hayter is to the right, with Traveller. Trooper was everyone's favourite; he often sat up like a cat with his front legs in the air.

AN EARLY COMBINE HARVESTER at Big Sands Field, Teffont. Taken in around 1946 at Manor Farm, our photograph shows the machine being pulled by an International crawler, model T35, which ran on TVO (Tractor Vapourizing Oil).

41

A TITAN TRACTOR at Sutton Mandeville in May 1925. Taken at Manor Farm, our picture shows some of the farm labourers employed by William Miles: M. Thick; J. Hardiman; F. Cross; A. Mullins; W. Thick; F. Thick; H. Johnson; B. Gunstone; and C. Cannon.

A FARMING SCENE at Fovant in the 1920s, with the famous Fovant Badges creating some additional interest in the background. The horses are pulling a hay sweep through the field, and on the other side of the picture an elevator is pitched up against a rick.

THE FIRST TRACTOR in Broad Chalke, 1919. The Fordson is pictured here pulling a binder across Bury Hill Field with Percy Harris at the controls. The machine had just arrived from the USA and Percy remembers that only one other man at Chalk Pyt Farm had driven the machine before him.

FEEDING CATTLE AT GURSTON FARM, Broad Chalke. Hubert Emm is pictured at the wheel of a 1959 Fordson Major tractor and his nephew, Trevor Morgan Emm, can be seen forking mangolds off the trailer.

TIME FOR LUNCH in a South Newton field in around 1899. Cecil Henstridge is sitting on the hay rake and Charles Down, Mrs Candy and Bill Thorne stand close by. Sitting around the picnic basket in front are Mrs Thorne, her two nieces and Lily Candy. In the group to the right are Ethel Ingram, Jack Thorne, Margaret Henstridge, Ethel and Annie Thorn, and Arthur Candy.

COLD TEA, fresh bread and Cheddar cheese. Four of Henry Swanton's lads taking a well-earned break at Manor Farm, South Newton, in 1939. Pictured to the left is Ronald Ansell, who prefered to drink his tea cold, then Frank Beckley, young Henry Henstridge and Bertram Williams.

MACPHERSON'S GARAGE, South Newton, on Good Friday 1922. William John MacPherson started off in the motor trade as a motorcycle engineer and then progressed on to other things, including car sales and coach tours. He retired in 1966. Many of our more senior motorists may remember having their petrol served by his wife Edith, whom he married in 1939. The garage has survived and a row of council houses has been built on the vacant land depicted to the left.

SHEEP SHEARERS at Steeple Langford in around 1914. Publican Henry Rowe and his wife stand at the door of the East End Inn, now the Rainbow's End. Sat on the bench with their well-deserved jugs of ale are John Whatley (nearest), 'Ted' Down, Tom Earley of Codford, 'Shep' Earley and George Whatley. The men had been sheep shearing at Eastcliffe Farm.

A TRAVELLING TWOSOME at Sutton Mandeville before 1910. Bill Targett and friend travelled all around South Wiltshire during the early years of this century carrying out all kinds of odd jobs in exchange for a hot meal and a good night's sleep in an outhouse or barn.

SIZING UP AN OAK at Grovely Wood after the Second World War. George Chalke of South Newton is to the right and Alec Dodson, his timber buyer, is to the left. The man calculating the hoppus measure is the representative of Truman, Hanbury Buxton & Co., brewer of Burton-on-Trent, who used the wood to make casks.

DINTON BRICK, TILE AND POTTERY WORKS in the nineteenth century. A wide range of goods were made here, including garden ornaments, flower pots, pedestals, water pipes, chimney pots, also plain and ornate house-building bricks.

A ROAD MAINTENANCE GANG at Fovant in the early 1920s. The men were carrying out general improvements to the Dinton Road. We believe that the steam road rollers were made by Aveling (left) and Marshall. Fred Mullins is the roadman second from the left.

BRIDGE WORK at Wilton in around 1929. James Whatley's building firm took on the job of widening Minster Street Bridge and laying new footpaths. There were at least seven men employed on the contract: Mr Brooks; Bill Dowding; Reg Fry; Pat Hibberd; George James; Fred Rixon and Ernie Ware.

STONELAYING near Fugglestone Crossroads during the First World War. The Burrell traction engine, *Masterpiece*, was commandeered by the War Department for urgent government work. Formerly it was used by John Cole, the amusement caterer, for towing fairground rides and living vans, and generating the power for his roundabouts. The photograph clearly shows the large slabs of granite that the labourers had to break down into smaller pieces before it could be rolled into the surface. We can only name two of these workmen; Albert Burden and his son 'Bill' can be seen by the nearside road wheel.

PUTTING THEM UP, maintaining them, and knocking them down. The picture above depicts some of the local men who were taken on before the First World War to erect the army huts at Fovant Camp. We have identified a few of them: Charlie Andrews; George Andrews (carpenter); Sid Barter; Ernie Blick (carpenter); Hubert Dibben; Reg Dimmer; Morgan Emm; Jim Foyle; Harold Trowbridge and Bert Young (plumber). Even after the building contract was completed a few civilian labourers were kept on to help the soldiers maintain their camp. Certain tasks like shoeing horses, however, were chiefly undertaken by military personnel. This is illustrated by the upper photograph on the next page which shows the 56-Battery farrier's shop. When the war came to an end some of the lads were taken on again to help dismantle the very same huts that they had built a few years earlier. The picture to the right, taken at Fovant Camp on 9 May 1921, shows one of the demolition gangs crowded around a War Department Foden Steam wagon.

FOVANT CAMP BLACKSMITHS.

THE DEMOLITION GANG.

STOP ME AND BUY ONE. Do you recognize the two characters pictured near the Railway Tavern at Hanging Langford in the 1950s? Even the Old Picture Detective could not solve the mystery of who they are.

PIG CARCASSES hung at Burcombe Mill. George Spearing can be seen here in this publicity photograph which was taken in around 1910. The wording on the board is just visible, 'These Pigs were fed on our Famous Meal'.

Post Offices, Pubs and Provisions

THE WYNDHAM ARMS HOTEL, Dinton, in 1884. Thomas Jukes was manager here when this picture was taken by Revd Edward Collett of Bowerchalke. This is the ideal place, perhaps, for us to explain how these very old photographs are reproduced in such a pleasing way. Revd Collett's contemporary print has faded to such an extent that most of the detail has virtually disappeared. The illustration above was created from the original by the writer who has enhanced the image. It really is a great improvement.

THE BISHOPSTONE BAKERY and general store, founded by John Compton in the 1850s and situated on the High Road near Pitts Lane. At the time of our photograph John's son Albert was managing the business. A fine selection of goods is displayed in the window. Two-gallon packets of Eiffel Tower lemonade powder can be seen, also Hudsons extract of soap, Quaker rolled oats, Reckitts Blue, Fry's pure cocoa, and Lyons tea. Before 1914 the business was transferred to the corner of Pitts Lane, and by 1925 it had been sold to F. Bailey & Sons of Broad Chalke. This is now a private dwelling named Pitts House.

BROAD CHALKE STEAM BAKERY and general warehouse. Established by Frank Bailey in the nineteenth century, the firm traded as E.F. Bailey & Sons. Over a period of many years, branches were opened at Bishopstone, Bowerchalke, Ebbesbourne Wake and Sixpenny Handley. This is now Holly Cottage and The Girnel.

BROAD CHALKE STORES and post office before 1890. To the left of our picture is John Hitchings, proprietor of the business from 1874 until 1897, when he moved to Knapp Farm. Telecommunications came late to this village; before 1895 the nearest telegraph office was at Dinton.

BOWERCHALKE POST OFFICE at the time of the First World War. Isaac Habgood Junior stands to the right, with his daughter Kathleen. A photograph of the Habgood family in earlier times has been reproduced on p. 12. We do not recognize the postmen here, do you know who they are?

THE BELL INN, Bowerchalke, early this century. Elizabeth Habgood had been a beer retailer in the village since the 1850s, but by the time of our photograph Isaac Habgood was licensed to sell beer, cider and tobacco from here. He can just be seen in the right foreground, near the pony and trap.

BOWERCHALKE SHOE SHOP and grocery store, before the First World War, showing Emily Penny and her daughter Kit. William Penny (1859–1948) opened up a footwear shop on this site in 1886. General provisions were introduced at a later date and William's son Fred was the proprietor from 1926 onwards.

EBBESBOURNE WAKE POST OFFICE and village store in around 1907. Thomas Wright was the sub-postmaster. The till rang for the last time in the summer of 1990 when the business was closed due to a general decline in custom. The village is without a post office now for the first time in more than a hundred years.

SWALLOWCLIFFE POST OFFICE in around 1928. Ron Hope is the postman depicted here with a bicycle and Mary 'Polly' Burt (née Clarke) is the woman standing on the other side of the fence. Polly was sub-postmistress in the village from the closing decades of the last century until around the time of the Second World War. This is now a private residence known as The Old Post Office.

THE ROYAL OAK, Swallowcliffe, before 1910. The man standing at the door is probably William 'Bill' Hansford, who was the licensee at this time. The scene appears to be virtually unchanged today.

THE LONDON ELM INN, Swallowcliffe, in 1907. The hostelry closed in around 1914 and was converted into private residences, and for years afterwards all the dwellings along here were known as London Elm Cottages. The wagon in the picture was owned by farmer Cornelius James Hunt, who had travelled out from Manor Farm, Manston, Dorset.

THE CRIBBAGE HUT INN, Sutton Mandeville, in the late 1920s. Long since demolished, this was once a very popular place. Numerous landlords have come and gone over the years and a list follows of just a few of them: Thomas Foyle (1850s); Henry Goodfellow (1880s); Sidney Street (1900s); Allan Burton (1910s); and John Gauler (early 1920s). From around 1923 and through the 1930s, Albert Trulock Spencer was the publican and he can be seen in our picture with his wife and their pet poodle. The man standing with them is Harry Hardiman, who was the licensee of the Compasses Inn at Chicksgrove, near Tisbury.

THE SWEET SHOP at Sutton Mandeville in around 1918. Situated at Sutton Cross, this is now a private dwelling known as The Stables. The business was established before the First World War by Mr and Mrs Alfred Mullins. In the original photograph one can just see a tin of Crawfords biscuits displayed on the table under the canopy.

THE PEMBROKE ARMS AND CROSS KEYS at Fovant in 1917. Catherine Read was manager of the Pembroke Arms at this time, and the sign which can be seen on the sheds in the background would suggest that she also hired out cars and carriages. The soldiers are standing outside Edwin Perrett's hostelry, The Cross Keys.

FOVANT STORES. This was not Albert Jukes's only shop: a trade directory of 1907 suggests that he also ran the village stores at Compton Chamberlayne. The MacFarlane poster, which can just be seen to the left of the shop window, was printed in 1908.

THE KING'S ELM INN, Compton Chamberlayne, in around 1916. The mounted Australasian soldier (a sergeant) had probably ridden into the village from one of the nearby military camps. The pub has closed and this is now a private house.

COMPTON CHAMBERLAYNE POST OFFICE in 1907. The sub-postmistress at the time was Mrs Annie Plowman. The building, which can still be seen on the main Salisbury–Shaftesbury road, is now three private dwellings: Postman's Cottage, October Cottage, and Old Post Office Cottage.

BURCOMBE POST OFFICE in 1906. The lady pictured here is thought to be Caroline Louisa Hibberd, the wife of the sub-postmaster, James Bailey Hibberd. Situated across the main road from St John's church, this is now a private residence known as Church Cottage.

THE SHIP INN at Burcombe. On 17 November 1917 a note was pencilled on the back of the original picture: 'Girlie Dearest, This little place is on the way to Wilton. The inn, known to everyone as 'The Ship', is about the most interesting place there, but havn't been inside of it yet.' Signed 'Brian, No. 3 Command Band, Hurdcott Camp, Wilts.'

BARFORD ST MARTIN POST OFFICE in around 1930 when Mrs Snook was managing the business. Situated in West Street, this is now a private house known as Fern Cottage. The last post office to operate in this village was finally closed in March 1990.

GERRY'S OF DINTON in 1927. John Cuff started trading as a baker and grocer in the nineteenth century and it was not until 1926 that Charles Henry Gerry took on the business. George William Stokes was the proprietor in the 1930s. Pictured here with his brother Rex is Lloyd Gerry, who returned to the shop after the Second World War.

DINTON POST OFFICE after the First World War. The sub-postmaster at this time was William Wyatt, who was a very active individual. He was organist at Compton Chamberlayne and Baverstock, captain of the Dinton Bellringers, a member of Dinton Choral Society, and a practised thatcher. William's son, John, can be seen here outside the post office with his sister Elsie. The building, which has since been demolished, was situated on the southern side of the main road, just down from Dinton Stores. John Wyatt passed away on Boxing Day 1990, in his ninetieth year.

TEFFONT EWYAS POST OFFICE and boot stores in 1905. The sign on William Thomas Brooks's shop reads: 'Cash Draper & Grocer. Boot and Shoe Stores.' Mr Brooks was formerly a shoemaker at Dinton and his wife, Catherine Jane, ran the post office at Teffont. These are now private cottages known as Brookly and Three Hands.

THE BLACK HORSE at Teffont in around 1925. It was rebuilt after being destroyed by fire some years earlier. At the time of our photograph the hostelry was owned by the People's Refreshment House Association, PRHA.

THE RAILWAY INN, Hanging Langford. When Walter Witt took over the pub licence in 1913/14 he would not have thought that his wife Annie would still be serving behind the bar some fifty-two years later. Annie retired in 1966 and died not long afterwards at seventy-five years of age. The young lad pictured here is Eric Witt. In 1989 this eighteenth-century inn sold for more than £160,000.

THE BOOT INN at Berwick St James. In 1911 George Feltham Keel was the landlord. The wagon depicted here is loaded with coal and a pair of sack trucks. Where could the carter be? Tom Kitley can be seen cycling up High Street.

THE BELL INN at Steeple Langford just before the Second World War. Fanny Elizabeth Florance was the keeper. The inn stands empty at the time of writing and several 'Pub to Let' signs are fixed to the building. When this photograph was taken in 1939, however, things were quite different: the pub was a very popular place, not just with local people, but also with motorists using the A36. The Austin motor car (AYA 972) was up from Somerset and the one behind it (WV 9091) was from a neighbouring village. The latter was a Bedford 2-ton lorry owned by Gilbert Davis Smith, the Wylye-based coal and timber merchant and haulage contractor. His telephone numbers were painted on the cab doors, numbers 21 and 22.

TRIANGLE POST OFFICE, Stapleford, before 1920. Post Office Cottage was demolished many years ago because of its precarious situation. It stood on the triangular plot of land which is located at the Stapleford turning off the A36 trunk road. Walter Waterman was the sub-postmaster.

SOUTH NEWTON POST OFFICE in around 1909. Mrs Elizabeth Jane Plowman and Arthur can be seen here in the garden. This is now a private residence known as 1 Knew Cottages. The earliest known transfer of the property took place in 1860 when all four cottages were sold for £100.

THE SWAN INN, Stoford, in 1920. The most distant part of the building was destroyed by fire some time before the First World War and was later reconstructed by R. Moulding, builders of South Newton. Edward Tabor was the publican when this picture was taken.

THE BELL INN at South Newton in 1897. The lady standing at the door is probably Mary Green, who was the publican here at the time. A decade before, however, the registered keeper was Peace Green, of whom we know very little.

THE ROYAL OAK at Great Wishford. Very few changes have taken place here since this delightful picture was taken around eighty years ago. If the horse-drawn phaeton had not been here and we could not see the style of the clothes that these people are wearing, then the photograph could have been taken yesterday.

Churches and Chapels, Schools and Societies

SALISBURY II at Bowerchalke in 1887. This is the second of the Church Army caravan missions which toured Wiltshire for the purposes of promoting religion. An organ and various other musical instruments were carried, as well as an abundant supply of temperance literature which was distributed during the services held mostly for the working classes. The photograph was taken by Revd Edward Collett.

STRATFORD TONEY VICARAGE in 1906. This was the residence of Revd Alfred Ralph Wilson, rector of the parish from 1903 to 1913, when he was succeeded by Revd Frank Edward Bignold. After standing empty for some considerable time the house was restored and, in 1926, it became the home of Colonel Charles S. Collison DSO. It is now known as Stratford Tony House.

SUTTON MANDEVILLE RECTORY in 1889. Bob Cross and Burt Riggs are the gardeners pictured here on the lawn in front of the house. Revd John Wyndham was rector of this parish from 1840, Revd Guy Julian Bridges from 1889, and Thomas Heathcote Wyndham from 1904.

DINTON NATIONAL SCHOOL in 1907. The building was constructed of Dinton bricks and paid for by voluntary contributions at a cost of more than £875. The site was given by the Earl of Pembroke and the work was completed by 1875. At the time of our photograph John Vincent was the master, Mrs Lucy Croome was the infants' teacher, and an average number of 109 pupils attended. The maximum permitted would have been 130. Bill Pomeroy, third from the left, is pictured here with his school chums.

SUTTON MANDEVILLE SCHOOLHOUSE in around 1900. The teacher's residence is the part of the building which faces us and the classroom can be seen extending away from it to the right. Access to the schoolroom was through the white gates. Miss Roper and Betty Cross are pictured here.

GROVELY WOOD NATIONAL SCHOOL AND CHAPEL, erected in 1867 by the 13th Earl of Pembroke. Miss Kate Lampard was the school mistress during the closing years of the last century, when she was teaching a daily average of just twelve pupils. By 1903 the children were attending the school at Barford St Martin.

WISHFORD SCHOOL COUNTRY DANCE TEAM, 1925, with the church of St Giles in the background. The young ladies processed through the village on Oak Apple Day, proudly showing off the trophies that they had won during the previous few months. Christine Mundy (now Mrs Alec Moulding) and Rosa Butler are at the head of the parade, with Jane Bryant and Doris Bennett following on behind. Schoolteacher Miss Edith Mundy can be seen to the left.

STOFORD METHODIST CHAPEL AND SCHOOLROOM on 16 October 1912, the day of the official opening. In regular use until just a few years ago, the chapel was finally closed due to a general decline in the size of the congregation. In December 1987 the premises were sold for around £53,000 and converted into a private residence.

THE WORKING PARSON of Ebbesbourne Wake. The Revd Cecil North Arnold can be seen working near Fifield Bavant church, assisted by a man and two ladies who we believe to be Miss Nora Best and Miss Dorothy Allen. The photograph was taken before 1935.

A GATHERING at Ebbesbourne Wake Congregational chapel in July 1932. Pictured left to right: Mrs Albert Young; Charlie Andrews; Mr Kirkham (the minister, who lived at The Manse, Broad Chalke); George Dimmer; Mrs Kirkham; Mrs George Dimmer; Mrs Charlie Andrews; Derek Chubb; Mrs Amy Young; Tiny Vincent; Bess Vincent; Charlie Vincent; Mrs Peter Hardiman; Mrs Lily West; Mrs Hull.

THE JUNIOR CLASS at Bishopstone School, 1922/3. Left to right, top row: Myrtle Foyle; Fred Humphries; Ted Compton; -?-; Jessie Morland; Joe Brown; Ethel Wareham; Bert Coleman; and -?-. Middle row: Olive Ester; Molly Wareham; Kathleen Smith; Amy Dimmer; -?-; and -?-. Kitty Wheeler, Frank Foyle, Leslie Webb and Maisie Kent are at the front. The teacher is Miss Searle (later Mrs Marks).

THE BISHOPSTONE SCHOOL MAYPOLE DANCE TEAM in 1906. From a photograph taken by William Jukes.

STANDARDS II AND III at Bowerchalke School, 1909. Thomas Hyde Penfound was head teacher here from the time of our picture through to 1915, when he married Miss Prescilla Aldwynckle by special licence and moved away to Berkshire.

THE MAYPOLE DANCERS of Dinton School in 1907. Police Sergeant Briant and headmaster John Vincent are to the left of the picture and Mrs Lucy Croome, the infants' mistress, is to the right. Among the girls we can see Florrie Moody, May Burton, Hilda Bert, Agnes Jukes, Eadie Lane, Winnie King, Helen King, Ada Lane, Hilda Baker, Daisy Galliett, Muriel Tinham, Lucy Jukes, Molly Jukes, Dolly Watley and Dora Lane. The author acknowledges the help of Mrs Florence Read (née Moody) who was able to donate this delightful picture with the names of her school friends shortly before she passed away in June 1991.

BROAD CHALKE SLATE CLUB DAY in around 1903. Club Secretary Arthur Penny marches at the head of the procession with Fred Drewitt beside him carrying the banner. After grouping at Manor Farm, the members attended a thanksgiving service at All Saints church before marching back to the farm where they enjoyed a hearty meal.

BOWERCHALKE CLUB MEET at Whitsuntide. After they had gathered at John Coombs's farm the men attended an eleven-o'clock service at Holy Trinity church. From here they marched to Williamson's barn at Knowle where they were greeted by a wonderful spread which had been prepared by the women of the village.

FOVANT BAND at the Cribbage Hut in the 1920s. The following individuals can be seen here: Reg Thick; Alfred Mullins; Tommy Riggs; Albert Spencer (the publican) and his wife; Alfred Lever; Frank Lever; Ted Hardiman; Frank Targett; Wilfred Target; Alfred Lever Junior; Bill Coombes; Fred Coombes and Margaret Mullins.

WISHFORD OAK APPLE DAY, 29 May 1950. With the Royal Oak Inn as a backdrop, Eric Mundy can be seen carrying the Union Flag at the head of the procession, and Monty Pearce and Percy Ransome following on behind with the Oak Apple Club banner. Society Chairman Percy Mitchell and Secretary Len King appear in the middle of the group.

SOUTH NEWTON BRASS BAND at the Stone Hole before 1910. Left to right, in the back row: Charlie Blake; Harry Thorne; Harry Lodge; Ernest Everett; -?-; -?-; Lampard; Cecil Henstridge; and Mr Cooper. In the front: Arthur Candy; Jack Hayter; Frank Beckly; Arthur Plowman; Harry Pitt; and Harry Liney. The photograph was taken at the side of the Bell Inn.

DINTON FOOTBALL CLUB, 1921/2. Back row, left to right: B. Whatley; S. Wootton; R. Pearse (hon. sec.); E. Avery; W. Stokes; A. Jarvis; T.E. Jukes (chairman) and F. Winter. Middle row: W. Wheeler; S. Pittman (captain); A. Pomeroy and R.H. Baker. Front row: E. Juke; F. Wright; F. Coombes; J.R. Jukes and A. Love.

Scenes Around the Villages

STRATFORD TONY VILLAGE in 1916. During the early years of this century the cottages depicted here were occupied by many different families; Baker, Castle, Compton and Goddard to name just a few. St Mary's church cannot be viewed from the same spot today because of the large number of trees which have grown up around the Common.

CROUCHESTON MILL, Bishopstone. Sidney Kent was the water miller here between 1897 and 1922. A hard-working, industrious man, he and his wife Eliza raised fourteen children, all but one of whom can be seen on p. 13. The mill was accidentally destroyed by fire during the Second World War and was never rebuilt.

FLAMSTONE STREET, Bishopstone, in around 1912. The residence nearest to the camera on the right is thought to be Flamstone Cottage and in the middle distance, with a cart parked outside, is Lower Thatch. Wheelrights Cottage can be seen on the other side of the road.

BISHOPSTONE HIGH ROAD, before 1912, showing Netton House and the White Hart Inn. A contemporary directory of inhabitants names Major Ralph Heygate as the occupier of the house and George Read as licensee of the pub. In later years Mrs Wordsworth lived at Netton House. She was the widow of the 93rd Bishop of Salisbury.

NORTH STREET, Broad Chalke, at the time of the First World War, with the Queen's Head Inn to the left. Fanny Nightingale was host at this popular pub during the closing years of the last century, but by 1920 William Stevens was the licence holder. About thirty years ago the barn and farm cottages pictured to the right were demolished and replaced by the houses and bungalows known today as Doves Meadow.

FLORENCE STOKES at Faulston Tower in 1917. Four of these defensive structures were built around Faulston House in the fourteenth century. This is the sole survivor. It was converted into a dovecot very many years ago.

SOUTH STREET, Broad Chalke, before the Second World War. Reddish House can be seen through the gate to the left. This is presently the residence of Toyah Wilcox, television personality and pop singer. Gladys Gulliver, Margaret Emm, Elsie Goodfellow and Howard Andrews add life to the scene.

OLD RECTORY GARDENS, Broad Chalke. When this photograph was taken in around 1910 poet Maurice Hewlett occupied the residence known today as King's Old Rectory. In the very early 1930s the Burroughes lived here.

MEAD END, Bowerchalke, in 1910. Yew Tree Cottage is on the left and Little Merrington can be seen in the far distance. The horse-drawn water barrel was used to carry water to the animal troughs in the fields.

BINGHAMS FARMHOUSE, Bowerchalke, in around 1908. This was the home of Robert Williamson, the village motor-bus proprietor, farmer and watercress grower. His bus (AM 2709) was supplied by the Scout Motor Company of Salisbury in October 1912. It was garaged in the building which can be seen to the extreme right of our picture.

MISSELFORE, Bowerchalke, in 1906. This scene remains virtually unchanged, although we will probably never again see children playing in the road with hoops and sticks.

FARM COTTAGES at Fifield Bavant in around 1904. Known today as numbers 1, 2 and 3 Thatched Cottages, these dwellings were occupied by Manor Farm employees and their families.

THE BLACKSMITHS of Ebbesbourne Wake. The man pictured here with the cart and two horses is Albert Young, one of three blacksmiths who earned their living in the village at this time. It is not his smithy, however, that we can see in the background; this is where Tom Young's forge was to be found. Albert's workshop was situated by the side of the chapel and he lived at Sundial Cottage. Tom's house was known as Gawens. He lived there with his wife Fanny until the time of his death in March 1954, when he was in his ninetieth year. Fanny passed away at her new home in Avebury in November 1960, when she was eighty-nine years of age. The picture was taken before the First World War.

COMMON LANE, Swallowcliffe, taken from The Cross in 1907. The white house to the left has gone and a modern bungalow now stands here. The photograph was taken by Charlie May, who had probably pedalled all the way from his home at Porton. You can catch a glimpse of him with his bicycle on p. 19.

HIGH STREET, Fovant, after the Great War. The thatched dwellings to the left were known as Doomsday Cottages, where Mrs Wyatt and Bill Ewence lived at one time. Latymer House stands on the site today. The old National Stores is now the Handy Shop.

A PICTURE POSTCARD VIEW of Fovant in 1916 depicting Waterfall Cottages and the Soldiers Delight (an artificial lake). Long since demolished, the cottages were occupied at different times by Lacy Foyle, Jack Gray and 'Jobbie' Jay.

A WOODMAN'S COTTAGE at Compton Chamberlayne before 1914. John Wyatt (hurdle, spar and gad maker) is pictured here with his wife Sarah (née Card, of Donhead), his son William and grandson John. Another picture of the family appears on p. 11.

AN EDWARDIAN VIEW of Compton Chamberlayne. The photograph was taken in around 1907 when Albert Jukes was proprietor of the general store which is on the left. Forge Farm can be seen on the other side of the road. It was formerly a village smithy.

BURCOMBE VILLAGE in 1916. Walnut Cottage, left, was formerly the village alehouse and also the residence of Polly and Walter Gumbleton. The motor car is parked close to Ernest Saunders's post office. A large number of bats and owls inhabited Blue Barn, which can be seen to the right.

THE TINY HAMLET OF UGFORD, at the time of the First World War. The farm workers' dwellings pictured to the left have survived but the thatched cottages in the distance have gone.

BARFORD ST MARTIN ROLLER MILLS in 1903. During the closing years of the last century Alfred Gray was producing flour at this water mill, but by the time of our photograph Mrs Mary Gray and her son were the proprietors. This is now a private residence known as Mill House.

WEST STREET, Barford St Martin, at around the time of the First World War. Cross Cottage can be seen in the distance, home to at least three generations of the Hunt family. The old bakery is pictured to the left. The Australasian soldiers were probably from one of the military camps which were set up around Fovant.

DINTON RAILWAY STATION and the station master's house in 1884. Built on the Wilton and Tisbury section of the main London and South Western Railway line from Salisbury to Yeovil, which was opened on 1 June 1860. The station closed in the spring of 1966. In April 1990 it was featured in the property section of the *Salisbury Journal* and, although a firm price was not quoted, offers of £70,000 or more would have been considered. Walter Blount was the station master when Revd Edward Collett of Bowerchalke took this photograph.

DINTON WATER MILL in March 1907. The Bugg family operated the mill from the 1850s until around 1886 and Bernard Sanger was the miller here when the machinery finally ground to a halt in around 1900. At the time of our picture riverkeeper Walter Moody was living here, with his wife Emily and their children Florence 'Florrie' (later Mrs Jack Read) and Percy.

POST OFFICE CORNER, Teffont Magna, after the Second World War. Farmer Giles's dairy herd is pictured heading back to Fitz Farm, to the yard opposite the Reading Room. A Bedford 15 cwt MW-type army truck can be seen turning the corner.

HOME CLOSE, Teffont. Taken in the late 1930s, our picture features two of Albert Spiller's grandchildren. Mavis (now Mrs Lovell) and Jo (Mrs Brooks) can be seen here with a pet lurcher called Nip and a greyhound named Dandy (left).

LITTLE BATHAMPTON FARM HOUSE in 1925. Ann Challis Ashford (née Hilder), the wife of Edward James Ashford, is pictured here with her daughter-in-law Keturah. Edward and Ann came to Wiltshire in 1888 to manage Tedworth Farm, Tidworth. After twelve years they moved to Little Bathampton where they remained until retiring to the Mount at Wilton in 1930.

HANGING LANGFORD VILLAGE in 1906. The residences on the right of the picture are known today as Yew Tree Cottage and Peach Cottage, and the ones on the left are named Langlee, Jasmine Cottage and Witt House. The photograph was published by the village grocer, Thomas Smith.

STAPLEFORD VILLAGE in 1916. Pear Tree Cottage can be seen in the middle distance and Parsonage House is pictured to the left. The residence of Alfred Powell until around 1911, this was later the home of the Wallis family who worked Church Farm.

MANOR HOUSE, Hanging Langford, in around 1911. The people depicted here are probably Mr and Mrs Thomas Powell, who were working Manor Farm at the time, and Revd Oswald Holden. The photograph was taken by Albert Marett, who can be seen on p. 19.

HIGH STREET, Berwick St James, at the time of the First World War. The cottages to the right are known today as The Row, and they stand opposite Magna House. The Ford Model T delivery van which is pictured in the distance is parked close to Rose Cottage, Shepherd's Cottage and Old School House.

MANOR FARM HOUSE, Stapleford, in the 1920s. Frank and Rhoda (née Setter) Moore started farming here before the First World War and continued to do so until 1932, when Frank died at the age of sixty-nine. He is pictured here with Victoria and May, two of his eight children.

STOFORD BRIDGE in around 1921. It is said that the following words are engraved on the keystone above the middle arch, 'Rebuilt by Plowman and Jay, 1841'. The carter had probably driven into the river to soak the wheels of his waggon which had developed an annoying squeak.

VICARAGE ROW, South Newton, in around 1900. The six dwellings stood on the southern side of the main road, in a central position opposite the vicarage, St Andrews church and the reading rooms (now a residential bungalow). By 1935 the cottages had been condemned and some of the families were removed to new homes at Jubilee Terrace.

GREAT WISHFORD in 1903. Pictured here outside George Young's general store and post office is a group of about thirty children with their school mistress Mrs W. Hatfield. The photograph was taken by William Jukes, who can be seen on p. 22.

THE GREAT WESTERN RAILWAY STATION at Wishford in around 1905. Station master James Richings can be seen here on the original platform which was built on the single-tracked Salisbury to Warminster section, which was opened on 30 June 1856. The waiting-room and shelter on the left-hand side were provided later when the line was doubled.

Scenes Around the Town

WILTON, from Grovely Hill, 1898. The railway bridge at Ditchampton appears in the middle ground and beyond the chimneys at the felt mill and the carpet factory, and in the far distance one can just pick out the spire of Salisbury Cathedral. A comparative photograph could not be taken today because of all the houses which have been built around here.

THE HOLLOW in 1904. These brick, rubble and thatch cottages were well over two hundred years old when they were demolished in the early 1920s. One row of five similar units was sold privately in August 1919 after an attempt to sell them at auction had failed. The reserve on Lot number 23 was set at just £90.

THE OLD MARKET CROSS at the time of Queen Victoria's Diamond Jubilee. More than ninety years later some much needed repair work was carried out to the medieval market cross, thanks to Mrs Nancy Morland, mayor of Wilton 1990/1.

THE MARKET PLACE, showing the Wool Loft, Bank House and the home of woolstapler John Doling, who died in 1845. The buildings were demolished in the 1920s and the site is now the Market Place car park. Beyond the railings to the right, the thoroughfare known as Bread Street can be seen.

WILTON TOWN HALL at the time of the First World War. A new clock turret was donated by W.V. Moore Senior, retired mayor of Wilton, in memory of Queen Victoria's Golden Jubilee. Gas lighting was installed to illuminate the four new dials, which were unveiled in January 1889.

WEST STREET and Four Corners, before 1918. At number 53, to the left of the above picture, Charles Seymour Elliott's drapery and tailor's shop was to be found, and in more recent times, Wilton post office. Albert Whatley was a baker and grocer on the corner of North Street, where Midland Bank is now, and on the other side of the road the Misses Winter managed their newsagent's shop and lending library. Their neighbour was Frederick Snoad, a confectioner. One can see that the three-storey wool warehouse has 'Danger' signs and 'For Sale' posters fixed to it.

SOUTH STREET and Four Corners before 1918. Elizabeth Pretty was the sub-postmistress at Wilton post office, which is depicted here on the corner of West Street. The little jewellery shop next door was occupied by watchmaker Francis Clifford, and on the other side of the street William Read's carriage hire office was to be found.

NORTH STREET in 1931. An Albion lorry loaded with Golden Shred marmalade can be seen outside Barrett and Brown's shop, which is easily identified by the white horse on the roof. This building was formerly a malt house, where Thomas Holly brewed beer from 1864 until around 1910.

WEST STREET in around 1875, the earliest known photograph of this thoroughfare. In the distance one can pick out the toll house which was demolished in 1963, and to the left Mr W.V. Moore's premises and the Victoria Arms Inn are shown. The dwellings to the right were knocked down very many years ago, and at the time of writing some retirement flats are being built here.

ST JOHN'S ALMSHOUSES, West Street, in around 1880. The Hospital of St John was founded by Hubert, Bishop of Sarum (later Archbishop of Canterbury) in 1189. It supported two poor men and two poor women who each received 8s. (40p) a week. The prior was appointed by the Dean of Salisbury.

WEST STREET in 1915. Henry Page's drug store is depicted to the left, where Pemberton Somerville, the interior decorators, are today. Previously 47, this is now number 16. Two women can be seen gossiping outside The Wilton Arms Inn, now The Bear.

FORTY YEARS LATER. The Ford van parked outside Mr Morris's shop was owned by one of his competitors, Snooks the butcher and grocer of 9 Butcher Row, Salisbury. The shop is now closed but the name R.C. Morris can still be seen on the blue and white tiles below the window.

WILTON NATIONAL SCHOOL in 1907. Situated in West Street, the school was built in 1842 to accommodate a maximum of 420 children. Residences for the master and mistress were also included. At the time of our photograph Leonard Hinton was the headmaster, Mrs Kate Stone was the mistress and Miss Kate Lloyd was the infant teacher. An average of three hundred children were attending. Financed by the Mayor's Appeal Fund, the school was converted in 1977 and is now Wilton Community Centre.

THE NEW INN AND WEST STREET BAKERY, 1890. The public house, bakery and grocer's shop were owned by Henry Street. The man pictured here in a white apron is Frederick 'Doughnut' Shergold, who was a baker at the Co-op for many years. A branch of Peter Dominic occupies the site today.

THE PEMBROKE ARMS FAMILY AND COMMERCIAL HOTEL, 1903, when Joe C. James was the manager. The local excise office was situated here many years ago and one can still see the words 'Inland Revenue Office' above the ground floor window on the right of our picture. Now known as Minster Cottage, the white-painted house in the distance was the hotel annexe.

JOHN WHITE'S PROVISION STORES, North Street, in around 1910. Mr White, depicted here wearing a white hat, was the proprietor of a chain of shops with the principal branches being at Tisbury and Wilton. The firm is well remembered for its unusual window displays, and perhaps one of the favourite promotional gimmicks to be seen at Wilton during the early years of this century was the ingenious electrical device created and supplied by the makers of Bovril. This fascinating optical illusion was known as 'The Bovril Ghost' and the following words should help you conjure up in your own minds an imaginary picture of this novelty: 'Shrine of the Mighty can it be, that this is all remains of me'.

FUGGLESTONE COTTAGES, King Street, in 1922. The Fry family occupied numbers 2 and 3 at this time. Our photograph shows Cecily Fry and her son Reginald. Cecily's husband, George, was a carter at Bemerton Farm.

MISS UPHILL'S DUGOUT in South Street. Pictured during the First World War, the premises were opened as recreational rooms for soldiers. The building was formerly a Quaker meeting house and later the Oddfellow's hall and Conservative Club. Wilton library can be found here today.

MISTER JUKES' WITHDRAWING ROOM. Edith Jukes is pictured here with Stella and Len, two of her seven children. Her son appears to be browsing through an album of family photographs, which in all probability contained numerous pictures taken by his father, Wilton photographer William Jukes.

THE WILTON ESTATE SAW MILL, as seen from the South Street Bridge over the River Wylye. Experienced hands were not too far away when these trees needed lopping in 1928. The residents of South Street frequently complained about the amounts of smoke which billowed out of the chimney.

CORONATION DECORATIONS in North Street, 1953. The shop proprietor at the time was Bessie Partridge (née Pike), who married Alfred Partridge after the death of her first husband, Harry Blake.

WILTON FELT MILLS before November 1905. The building to the left is the oldest surviving part of the works. Turn to pp. 34 and 35 to see some interior views of the factory. The foreman's house can be seen in the distance. It was occupied by the Foyle family who are pictured on p. 22.

THE LONDON AND SOUTH WESTERN RAILWAY STATION in around 1900. This was situated on the main Salisbury/Yeovil section, which was opened in June 1860. Charles Tancock was the station master during the closing years of the last century. He lived with his wife Rebecca at Pembroke Terrace.

THE GREAT WESTERN RAILWAY STATION in around 1904. It was on the Salisbury and Warminster branch of the Wilts, Somerset and Weymouth Railway (later GWR), which was opened on 30 June 1856. Edward Miller was station master at this time and he lived at Bilbury Cottage.

A WILTS AND DORSET DOUBLE-DECKER in the Market Place. In March 1921 these passengers had arrived from Salisbury on the new 2A service via Harnham Bridge. Their conveyance, a Brush-bodied forty-five seater, was based on an AEC YC-type chassis, with registration number CD 2555. A very basic machine, it had solid tyres, an open top deck and open cab. The bus is partially obscuring our view of the site upon which the wool loft had stood some weeks earlier. On the south side of the square, where The Duck Next Door can be found today, George Bell traded as a saddler and harness maker.

NORTH STREET after the flood, February 1937. Gilbert Lever's butcher's shop can be seen on the extreme left of our picture. This was number 18 at the time, but became number 39 later on. Reginald Lewry's drapery business occupied numbers 19–20, and Cecil Earle was a cycle dealer at number 21, a close-up of which is reproduced on p. 129. A GWR Thornycroft lorry can be seen passing a stationary Ford, which is in the colours of Messrs Wort and Way.

THE SIX BELLS INN, North Street, decorated by publican Frank Pike on the occasion of the Relief of Mafeking. His wife Emma can be seen in the doorway and his daughter Bessie is standing to the right, wearing a white apron.

THE WHEATSHEAF INN at the time of the First World War. Tom Everall can be seen at the door of the pub which he ran from 1917 to 1927. He was a keen hunter and follower of the Wilton hounds. His horse was kept in the stables which are just out of view to the left.

MOORE BROTHERS' WORKSHOPS at Ditchampton in around 1924. The business was established here soon after the First World War by Henry and William Moore, the sons of William Vincent Moore Junior. For many years the brothers were agents for the Wolseley Motor Company of Birmingham, although they also carried out general repairs to many other types of motor vehicles. The Wolseley tourer in our picture has a Somerset registration, YA 5704. We believe also that the first electric petrol pump in the town was installed here. John Moore, Henry's son, is the proprietor at the present time.

Right: WILTON WATER WORKS in around 1906. The pumping station and chimney have gone, but the chief engineer's house can still be seen at Water Ditchampton. A private dwelling now, it is appropriately named Water House.

THE TALBOT AND WYVERN COFFEE TAVERN, 24 Kingsbury Square, in the 1920s when F.W. Musselwhite was the manager. It was a busy place and the meeting rooms were hired out regularly to numerous local societies. The billiard room was naturally very popular. A private dwelling known as Wyvern House stands on the site today.

AT YOUR SERVICE. The Barrett and Brown grocery shop, which opened at 13 North Street during the 1920s, served the people of Wilton admirably for more than two decades. The firm achieved an enviable reputation and their customer base stretched far and wide. We believe that Mr Mould is the white-haired man to the left of the group.

OUT ON THE ROUNDS. The driver of this 1927 Morris Commercial van was delivering a wholesale order to Ralph Parker's shop at Codford.

EARLE'S SHOPS, at 21 and 22 North Street, in around 1930. Harry Earle started a wholesale confectionery business at 92 Milford Hill, Salisbury, in around 1890, and by 1905 he had opened his first retail shop at 30 Catherine Street. The Wilton outlets were introduced later: by 1920 Cecil George Earle was managing a motor and cycle engineering business at 21 North Street, and his wife Mable Annie, née Hinton, was a confectionery retailer at number 22. By 1935, however, the sweet shop had closed, and later still radios were being sold for the first time. Eventually, Cecil handed the business over to his son Anthony, who in the course of time established himself as an antique dealer. And it is Anthony's widow, Betty, who is the proprietor of Earle's today.

THE WILTON ROYAL CARPET FACTORY in 1948. Shown here are the nine women who put the finishing touches to the carpet which was made especially for the lower foyer of the Empire Theatre, Leicester Square, London. Woven in one piece, it measured 23 foot 4 inches by 39 foot 6 inches.

WILTON RECREATION GROUND. This leisure park was set out in 1911 on a site formerly known as the Hop Ground. The land had to be leased from the Earl of Pembroke. Frederick Charles Blake is the groundsman pictured here in the early 1920s.

THE MAGDALEN ALMSHOUSES in 1928, known today as the Magdalen Trust Houses. The following inscription can still be seen on the building: 'This hospital of Saint Mary Magdalen of Wilton was rebuilt on its present site in fulfilment of the intentions of George Augustus Earl of Pembroke and Montgomery by Catherine his widow and sole Executrix. AD 1831.'

WILTON CROSSROADS in the 1930s. The large AEC van is in the livery of the London & Southern Counties Transport Company, whose local depot was at the rear of 27 West Street. Their fleet of vehicles carried the legend 'Spans the South' and even today, some fifty years later, local people can easily remember 'Spans'.

THE WILTON ROAD at around the turn of the century. A great number of trees in the area were uprooted during a most violent storm in January 1930.

SECTION EIGHT

Memorable Events

CELEBRATING THE DIAMOND JUBILEE of Queen Victoria at Wilton. On Thursday 24 June 1897, the mayor, Mr John Montague Swayne, addressed a huge assembly of local adults who had gathered in the Market Place to enjoy a midday banquet. At three o'clock in the afternoon around six hundred children were entertained to tea at the same tables. The sun shone brightly all day and not a single cloud was to be seen in the sky.

THE INAUGURATION of the Wilton memorial fountain, 31 July 1901. The drinking fountain was placed on the corner of The Avenue, close to Wilton Cross Roads, as a memorial to the Earl of Pembroke who died six years earlier. Some time later, however, it was removed to the recreation ground where it stands to this day. Manufactured from Portland stone by Messrs Farmer and Brindley of London, the monument has an inside diameter of 10 feet. The following inscription can still be seen around the bowl, 'This fountain is given by Gertrude Countess of Pembroke in memory of happy days at Wilton. Trusting that it will be a comfort to all passers by and thirsty animals. 1901 AD.'

WILTON SPRING FAIR, 1903. There were two major fairs held in the town each year. The spring fair, which was usually held on 4 May, was for horses, cattle and sheep, and the autumn fair was principally for sheep only, and this habitually took place on 12 September. A charter was granted and the first Wilton sheep fair was held in 1436.

BEATING THE BOUNDARY FESTIVAL at Wilton, 1905. A contemporary report of the event was never found, despite a thorough search by the Old Picture Detective. We can reveal, however, that the 'Car of the Children' won first prize.

THE FUNERAL OF LORD CLANWILLIAM, 8 August 1907. Born in 1832, the late peer was first cousin to the Earl of Pembroke, his mother being a daughter of the 11th Earl. The cortège is pictured in North Street *en route* to Wilton parish church where the Earl's body was laid to rest close to those of his parents who are interred there.

WILTON AFTER THE SNOW. On 25 April 1908 a most violent snowstorm swept across the south of England. This was the heaviest fall since the great storm of January 1881. A chilling wind blew persistently for more than twelve hours and huge drifts were formed in the more exposed places. It was a breathtaking sight to behold.

THE KING AND QUEEN at Wilton, June 1908. Their majesties had arrived at the L&SWR station at Salisbury after travelling from Waterloo in a Royal Special, and once the Salisbury civic formalities were concluded the king and queen departed for Wilton in a horse-drawn landau. The procession, which had progressed rather slowly along Wilton Road, broke into a trot after crossing Skew Bridge and arrived at Wilton almost exactly on time. The cavalcade stopped just short of Wilton Park gates where the mayor, Mr John Swayne, presented the king with an address of welcome. The mayoress having been introduced, Mr Swayne held up his pretty little daughter, Mina, while she handed to her majesty an exquisite bouquet of blooms known as the 'Princess of Wales'. The queen appeared extremely pleased and smiled most lovingly as she took the child's hand in her's amid tumultuous cheering. The picture above was taken on the following day, when the gracious couple attended Wilton parish church.

WINSTON CHURCHILL at Chiselbury Camp in 1910. Several well-known officers were involved with the military exercises that commenced on Monday 19 September. Field Marshall Earl Roberts and General Sir John French attended the camp from their headquarters, which was set up at the County Hotel in Salisbury, and the Duke of Connaught arrived each day by motorcar from The Cliffe at Harnham.

SOLDIERS and more soldiers. It was quite an unsettling experience for the local inhabitants as the movement of troops around Salisbury Plain continued twenty-four hours a day for five days. The rumble of airships, aeroplanes and motors could be heard during the day, and the sound of marching soldiers disturbed the peace of night.

A ROYAL PROCLAMATION at Wilton, Monday 9 May 1910. The mayor of Wilton, Mr George Bell, can be seen announcing the accession to the throne of King George V. He is accompanied on the steps of the Old Market Cross by Canon Olivier and the retired mayor, Mr John Montague Swayne.

CHRISTMAS FLOODS at Wilton, 1910. The raised timber planks around St John's Square had been provided by William Musselwhite, the borough surveyor, who also hired a horse-drawn conveyance to take people through the deep floodwaters along Water Ditchampton. This picture was taken on Friday 23 December.

CORONATION CELEBRATIONS at Wilton on 22 June 1911. The mayor and corporation joined more than 1,200 men and their lady-friends for a midday feast in the Market Place. Together they consumed over 900 pounds of meat (beef, mutton, veal and ham), 500 pounds of plum pudding and around 300 gallons of ale and mineral waters.

THE CORONATION PROCESSION, Thursday 22 June 1911. At about 1.45 p.m. the mayor and corporation left the Town Hall and joined the cavalcade, which can be seen in the photograph as it proceeded along West Street to the parish church. The Alliance Order of Oddfellows was at the head of the parade, followed by the South of England Prize Band.

THE FUNERAL OF LORD PEMBROKE, 7 April 1913. Sidney Herbert, 14th Earl of Pembroke and Montgomery, died in Rome on 30 March. The cortège is pictured here in South Street, where many distinguished people had gathered to pay their last respects. The coffin bearers were employees of the Wilton Estate.

A MILITARY FIELD KITCHEN at Wilton in May 1914. The picture effectively portrays the scene behind the B Lines of the North Somerset Imperial Yeomanry training camp. Numerous cooking utensils and a plentiful supply of coal can be seen here near the tents that were set up on Grovely Down.

WILTON UNDER WATER in 1915. John White is pictured here, second from the right, with members of his shop staff who had turned out in their wellington boots so that Mr Jukes could take this memorable photograph. His picture illustrates quite clearly that the flood water was only 3 to 6 inches deep on the corner of Crow Lane and North Street. The situation was much worse along West Street and Water Ditchampton, however, where Reginald Ford of the Bell Inn had recorded a depth of 18 inches in one of his bars.

THE PRINCE OF WALES at Wilton on Wednesday 23 May 1923. The royal Rolls-Royce landaulette can be seen passing hundreds of children from Wilton national school, who had assembled in an enclosure in the Market Place. In spite of heavy rain the town looked very gay with its decorated streets and buildings.

UNVEILING AN INSCRIPTION on the Pembroke memorial, 21 May 1924. 'This Site was acquired and This Monument erected by Public Subscription as a Memorial to Sidney, 14th Earl of Pembroke and Montgomery PC, GCVO, JP. Born 1853, died 1913.' The memorial has since been removed from Wilton Market Square and is now believed to be in a council store.

THE WILTON FLOOD of 1937. Taken on Tuesday 9 February, this photograph shows a team of council workmen helping out and tidying up around Water Ditchampton, which was flooded along its whole length. The council lorry is a 30 cwt Dennis (WV 83). Robert Sinca's grocery store is now a Spar shop.

WILTON OLD CHURCH being re-hallowed, 6 May 1939. The ceremony was performed in the presence of, among others, the Mayor of Wilton (Miss Edith Olivier), the Bishop of Salisbury (Dr Neville Lovett), and the Rector of Wilton (Revd Guy Ronald Campbell).

A PEACETIME PARADE. No precise date is available for this photograph, but it was certainly taken soon after the Second World War. Perhaps the women in uniform had taken part in a thanksgiving service at Wilton parish church.

AN ELIZABETHAN PAGEANT at Wilton in 1953. The part of Queen Elizabeth I was played by Miss Mary Shergold (later Mrs Hawley). Her ladies-in-waiting were Mrs Joan Ford and the Misses Phyllis Turner (Mrs Dredge), Eileen Bryant (Mrs Casley) and Sheila Payne. Charles Primmer was a yeoman.

Transport

AN EARLY FLYING MACHINE at Fovant. This Farman aeroplane was one of several to be seen around South Wiltshire during the military manoeuvres which took place in September 1910. Flown regularly by Captain Bertram Dickson, this biplane was powered by a 7-cylinder French-built Gnome engine. Its top speed was just 50 m.p.h.

STRATFORD TONY CYCLISTS, 1909. Sidney and Jane Gurd, pictured here in their front garden, were employed by Revd Alfred Ralph Wilson. Jane, who was christened Kezia Burgess, was cook and housekeeper at the rectory, and Sidney was the gardener and groom. They married in 1906.

THE ARNOLD FAMILY GOAT CART. Pictured here after 1892 is Revd Cecil North Arnold, his wife, and daughters Ruth and Dorothy. At first sight one could easily mistake this goat for a llama. Revd Arnold can also be seen on p. 78.

A DONKEY CART at Fovant Rectory: 'J.C. and M. at Fovant in 1907'. Sadly, the writer of this note did not record the full names of these delightful children. We can, nevertheless, reveal that they are the offspring of Revd Maitland Arthur Shorland.

A BUTCHER'S CART at Bowerchalke, in 1889. The man standing on the right, holding a joint of meat, is believed to be John Coombes. The picture was taken by Revd Edward Collett.

WISHFORD FOLK in a waggonette. This picture was probably taken at Grovely Wood in around 1900. When it was not 'Let out on Hire' this carriage was kept at livery stables in Wilton. On rainy days it could be sent out with a canopy fitted.

THE BROAD CHALKE BREAD CART, 1909. Charlie Knightingale is pictured here with his cart in Tank Lane, close to several cottages and barns, which have since been demolished. His bakehouse and shop was situated in South Street, opposite to where Fry's can be found today.

WILTSHIRE FARM WAGGONS at Wilton before 1914. The vehicles are parked outside the Wilton Arms Inn in West Street, the hostelry of Mrs Ann Eliza Ridout. It was generally known that she was pleased to serve carters, many of whom became regulars and stopped off at the pub each market day to enjoy a jug of ale.

THE COMPTON CHAMBERLAYNE CARRIER in around 1916. Joseph Langdon is pictured here with the cart that he used to deliver milk to the hospital huts at Compton Chamberlayne camp. He was the eldest son of William Langdon who farmed at Manor Farm from 1895 to 1920.

THE BISHOPSTONE VAN of the 1920s, pictured here at the White Hart garages. At the time of this photograph Cecil Wort was the operator of this Ford Model T carrier's bus and Alfred Fulford was the driver. It was garaged overnight at Bishopstone.

FROM EBBESBOURNE WAKE TO BOURNEMOUTH in the 1920s. For many years this Ford Model T waggonette was operated by Ernest Oborn, the Ebbesbourne Wake carrier. Taken near Sydenham's stationery shop at Pier Approach, this photograph shows Lizzie Habgood standing at the back, and Graham Oborn (Ernest's son) in the cab.

A LOCOMOTRICE, Rochet-Schneider of 1905. Assembled at the works of SA des Etablisse-
ments Rochet-Schneider of Lyons, France, but marketed by the Locomotrice Company of
Liège, Belgium. In April 1905 this 24 hp red-coloured side-entry model was purchased by
Richard Charles Baker, who was the lord of the manor of Hurdcott. This picture, taken at
Hurdcott House, shows 'James' the chauffeur with two lady passengers. At different times
Mr Baker ran numerous other cars including an early Scout, AM 892, a Daimler and a
Darracq.

A SCOUT COMBINATION of 1912. This very special Salisbury-built car, AM 2587, was just one of many fine motors owned by John White of Wilton. It had two interchangeable bodies: when the rear dickey seat was in the 'closed' position a useful goods-carrying platform was created at the back, or when the seat was 'open', as shown in the picture, the car was transformed into a five-seater. If a greater number of seats were required then the rear body section was removed altogether, and in its place a 'Tulip' passenger compartment was attached. The car would then seat seven quite comfortably, including the driver. The model aeroplane on the radiator filler cap is a nice feature.

THE 'YELLOW VICTORY' at Wilton in 1920. This Thornycroft forty-five seater was operated by the Salisbury and District Motor Services from April 1920 until August 1921 when the firm was acquired by Wilts and Dorset. Bert Jefferies, John White Junior, Arthur Cutler and Eric Blake are pictured with the vehicle.

JACK EMM'S PRIDE AND JOY, AM 6854, purchased by F. Bailey & Son in 1916. Based at Central Stores, Broad Chalke, this grey-coloured Ford Model T van was used to deliver provisions over a very wide area, including the army camps situated along the A30.

HOARE'S FORD. Some time during the early 1920s Leslie Hoare acquired the old, established business of Walter Burroughs, a grocer and baker of 81 North Street, Wilton. His ageing horse-drawn carts were quickly replaced with motor vans for the purposes of delivering bread and provisions around the district. There were at least two bread rounds: one took in Barford St Martin, Burcombe and Ugford; another encompassed Chilhampton, South Newton, Stoford and Wishford. The young lad sitting on the running board of this 1927 Ford Model T van is Albert Brice, who remembers that his wages were 7s. a week at first, plus a free lardy or dough cake on Saturday.

TESTING A TRIUMPH TWO-WHEELER. Registered in Wiltshire by the Secretary of State for War on 13 January 1916, this $3\frac{1}{2}$ hp Triumph motorcycle had a dark blue frame and a grey and green fuel tank. The picture was taken at the Wilton M.T. Depot.

AN ARMY AMBULANCE. In 1915 a fleet of nine Ford Model T ambulances was assigned to 348 Company, Motor Transport, Army Service Corps, Wilton. The batch was allocated registration numbers AM 5048 to AM 5056.

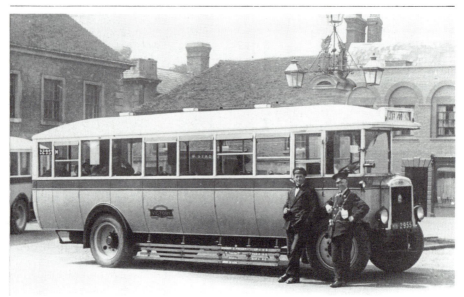

A VICTORY AT WILTON SQUARE, 1931. Messrs Sparrow and Vincent operated the Victory Motor Services from 1922 until they were taken over by the Wilts & Dorset company late in 1933. Pictured here with MW 2955, a Leyland PLSC3, is Charles John 'Charlie' Hoppé and William 'Billy' Ashford.

THE BEST VAN IN THE DISTRICT! Founded in 1867, the Wilton Sidney Herbert Co-operative Industrial and Provident Society Limited was situated at 10 Market Place. Albert Brice and Eddie Shergold can be seen here in South Street with the firm's Morris Commercial delivery van, which was supplied in 1931.